A Turn for the Worst

traumatic brain injury and a daughter's
search for answers

Robin Gentry McGee

This book is dedicated to my father, HP Gentry, who died just as he had lived, with grace, honor, and endless love. Also to my husband and the great love of my life, Brian McGee, who has stood firmly with me on this journey.

Contents

foreword

"Let Thy Food Be Thy Medicine and Thy Medicine Be Thy Food"
~Hippocrates

This story was written over the course of almost three years. While not every experience during this journey could be recorded, it is my hope to have provided enough information to be of some help to others that have loved ones facing similar injuries or illnesses.

The title of this book, *A Turn for the Worst,* is in my opinion, indicative of how very far away the medical profession has come from being healers, instead largely depending on drugs and other models that do not take the human spirit or the whole being into account.

The title also reflects what I heard over and over again during the course of my father's last days. When all of the drugs have failed and the human body is no longer able to sustain itself on the horrible substances that pass for food in most medical care facilities and the shift to death happens, many times the only explanation that loved ones ever receive is just that. "I am sorry, he took a turn for the worst."

I hope someone, somewhere, will find inspiration within these pages and realize it does not have to be this way.

One Sunny Morning

"Have you heard about Dad?" That was the first stunning question my brother would ask me. It was a question that would forever change my life, and the life of my entire family.

It was February 23, 2005, a brilliant and calm sunny morning. I was on my way to the gym. I had finally started to re-establish a consistent workout routine after having been vacant from my own life for well over three years.

I had previously owned a restaurant that specialized in organic whole foods, the first and only in the area, and it was a beautiful creation a gorgeous space with loyal, supportive customers. Yet the day-to-day difficulty of running a food service operation, as well as obtaining all-organic products was somewhat an exercise in futility. The restaurant took its toll on me both physically and mentally.

I had known many months earlier that I needed to take my curtain call but each time I informed my customers of my exit plan, they had the same reaction, "Oh no, but you can't!" Of course it *was* my responsibility not to let anyone down, so I continued on.

After one particularly grueling day, while driving home, I knew it was over. I was done. I told no one of my decision. I went in the following day, had a heart-to-heart with my employees, put a closed sign on the door, proceeded to liquidate, and walked away.

It was a highly difficult decision, but a necessary one. I felt as though I was letting my customers down, yet I had to choose to do this for my own personal survival. I was free. I had reclaimed the power to move forward and take steps to regain balance in my life.

One month later, I received the phone call. It was the day before my birthday.

"Have you heard about Dad? He slipped on the ice, hit his head, and is getting ready to undergo emergency surgery. His chance of survival is very small." HIS CHANCE OF SURVIVAL IS VERY SMALL. In that instant, my world began to rotate off its axis.

My father—my precious, loving, beautiful, generous father—my hero, was probably going to die. Just like that.

I remember screaming into the phone, "NO!! This is not happening!" I called the hospital, desperately trying to locate my mother, or anyone, who could tell me a mistake had been made. There was no mistake.

I frantically phoned my husband, who was at work an hour away. He raced home and we headed to Michigan, making the usual five-hour trip in three hours. We rushed into the emergency room.

He was already well into his surgery. I felt as though I was floating above my body, watching some gut-wrenching movie. All I could hear were the words "small chance of survival."

After what seemed like a lifetime of waiting, the surgeon came into the waiting room to speak with us. It was too soon to tell. It was a very bad brain bleed. He had suffered both an epidural and subdural hematoma. We could do nothing more than wait.

two

Left Waiting

My parents had been on their way to church when the accident happened. My dad, being the generous caretaker he had always been, insisted my mother wait at the door while he warmed the car before pulling to the door to pick her up. Apparently there was a patch of black ice next to his car, underneath his car door. When he opened the door, he slipped and his head went crashing into the doorframe.

At the time, it appeared to be just an innocuous fall. He proceeded to get into the car, picked my mother up, and casually told her, "I slipped and hit my head, but I'm okay." He drove to church, and while he was reading a passage from the Bible, started having trouble formulating his words.

My mother immediately took him to the emergency room. The doctor ordered an x-ray and a CAT scan and announced there was no damage. He was released to go home at noon on February 22nd.

About 3:00 a.m. the following morning, my father woke my mother and complained of a severe headache. He said he was having trouble with his vision. They immediately returned to the emergency room, where he sat for three hours in the waiting room. Three hours! A three-hour wait for a 75-year-old man, who was taking Coumadin, which is a blood thinner, and who had suffered a head injury!

Finally, he was taken into a room, where another CAT scan was performed. This time, they saw a severe bleed and decided to do emergency surgery. First they would need to thicken his blood due to the effects of the Coumadin he had been taking. However, there was no chance for the medical team to do this as my father lost consciousness, was intubated, and taken into surgery.

The last words my father spoke, according to my mother, before his life would change forever were "Forgive me, Father, if I have sinned."

To me or anyone who ever knew my father, it was unimaginable that he had sinned.

three

The Room

My father, a retired minister, as well as an accomplished musician, touched hundreds, if not thousands, of lives with his gentle spirit and kind heart. He lived his life to help others. Walking into his room in the critical care unit, I felt as though my heart was breaking into a million little pieces. I could not count the number of tubes hooked up to him. This could not be my father.

He was an amazing human being. He loved people, all people, and never met a stranger. I always was a little hesitant to go shopping with him, even on short trips to the market, because I knew what should be a five-minute stop would take much longer as he talked to everyone. I always joked that he would walk into a place and come out not only knowing everyone's name, but always with a few more friends to add to his ever growing list. He loved people deeply and sincerely and they loved him back. Young, old, and in between, he had a way of bringing a smile to everyone's face just by being present. That was my dad, a man who was always present and who had an incredible presence.

Now he was totally unconscious, comatose, but alive. All we could do was to wait and begin our vigil at the hospital.

My father is from a very large family, and I have three brothers. We were all there, taking turns going to sit with him. At one point, there were too many people to fit comfortably in the critical care waiting room. I had noticed a very comfortable-looking room that was kept locked next to the waiting room. I decided to ask a nurse if this room could be unlocked to accommodate everyone.

She told me that this particular room was the room where doctors took family members to tell them either that their family members had passed, or to ask them to make the decision to "unplug" their loved ones and let them go. She said, "You really do not want to go into 'the room,' if possible," and ended the conversation. I could not have been more in agreement.

Less than 48 hours after the first surgery, we were called into "the room."

The doctor delivered the news. He was bleeding again severely in his brain. They could either go in and try and stop the bleed or take him off life support.

"What are the chances of his survival if you operate again?" we asked. No one could say for sure. It was a critical situation. Someone said it would probably take a miracle. We believed in miracles and agreed to the second surgery.

My entire family gathered in his room before he was to be taken away for the second emergency surgical procedure in two days. None of us knew if we would ever see my father alive again, or if this would be our final goodbye. No one could speak of this, but it was what we all were feeling. Someone said a prayer and then someone else started singing *Amazing Grace*. I am from a family of singers and that is what we do; we sing. We sing when we are happy, we sing when we are sad, and we sing when someone leaves this earth to lift them up and carry them forth on the wings of a song.

He survived the second surgery. Due to the swelling in his brain, they removed part of his skull, giving his brain room to expand, and he was returned back to the critical care unit.

We remained at the hospital 24 hours a day. Only one person was allowed in his room at a time between the hours of 10:00 a.m. and 7:00 p.m. The rest of the time we gathered in the waiting room.

For weeks, he remained in a coma. The doctors never let us forget how critical the situation was and that his chances of regaining consciousness were very small.

Few of the doctors we encountered were capable of handing out hope. I remember one in particular whom I dubbed Dr. Death. I do not think he could have been any more negative.

I lost track of how many days we had been at the hospital. After a couple of weeks or so, I returned to Ohio for a few days to work, while my husband remained in Michigan. While I was home, I felt it imperative to start researching anything and everything on brain injury that I could find.

After some of the numbness wore off, I decided I must try to formulate a plan. If my father had any hope at all of survival, I was going to make sure we did everything that could be done.

four

Hope

"First Do No Harm"
~Hippocratic oath

I felt deep in my heart that, through integrative medicine, I would find more tools to offer my father for healing than Western medicine would, or could.

When I was not by his side, I spent every minute of every hour of every day on the internet. I searched for any information I could find on Traumatic Brain Injury (TBI). I read through hundreds of research papers and web sites, yet found very little practical information on the subject.

I did however find one website with information from a daughter who had walked with her mother through TBI. She too was given no hope, but she had refused to give up and developed a plan to bring her mother back to life. She had a step-by-step outline of things she did for her mother daily, such as reading the paper, telling her mother the day, month, and year. She would sit by her bedside and talk to her mother about the occurrences of her day, just as she had done for years. She always knew her mother could, on some level, hear her. This website provided exactly what I needed to find—hope. By the way, her mother had survived and had made steady progress toward recovery the last time I checked.

I was off and running. The first conversations I needed to have were with my father's doctors, other professionals, and anyone else who voiced their opinion on what a terrible condition he was in. It was simple. There would be no negative talk. The doctors and interns in particular seemed to bask in the ability to congregate around my father's bedside and discuss with each other just how poorly he was doing, while they stuck sharp needles under his fingernails and toenails to try and elicit some response.

I had found my voice and was not afraid to use it to tell everyone to take it outside.

We then proceeded to play his favorite music for him on a CD player we had brought into the hospital. My husband and I also decided that somewhere deep within him he could hear us. We began to sing to him, hoping that our voices and the music that he loved so deeply would somehow reach him.

The next step was getting him out of the coma. I thought through all I knew of Traditional Chinese Medicine (TCM). I knew there were specific emergency acupuncture points that were used to bring a person back to consciousness. I met with my acupuncturist in Ohio. She suggested finding a licensed acupuncturist in Michigan to bring into the hospital. My hopes soared at the possibility of something as tangible and significant as this. This hope was short-lived, for the hospital would not allow it. What next?

I had her show me the points, and even draw a diagram. First, I would start with acupressure using the blunt end of a pen. This advice came from another acupuncturist who was located in Michigan that my husband had met with in hopes of bringing her to the hospital. Although not possible due to "hospital policy," she provided us with some very valuable information. She too drew a detailed diagram *(See diagram 1)* of the acupressure points we were to use to stimulate his body for five minutes every hour, 24 hours a day. My husband and I took turns doing this.

If, after a couple of days, he still was not responding, I planned to actually try and engage the points myself, using lancets and working from the very detailed diagram. I had my husband learn this as well, knowing it would be difficult to stick lancets into my father and realizing that I really did not know what I was doing. I had no clue how I was going to manage this when my father's room was directly across from the nurse's station, but it was my father's life and I was willing to try anything. I knew that if we were caught, there was a possibility we would all be thrown out of the hospital, including my father. On some level, my father must have known the

Diagram 1

Bottom of feet, just under
the pad in the middle.

Under nose, just above
middle of the lips.

*The width of four of his
fingers down from the knee,
one thumb width to the outside over from the leg bone.
(both legs)*

trepidation I was feeling, because after the intermittent acupressure was
used to stimulate him for about 48 hours, he opened his eyes.

During this time, we had received word that one of my father's sisters had
passed. I truly do not believe in coincidences. It was the day of her funeral
and I had returned to Ohio to attend, wondering how much further into
darkness and despair I could sink. On top of her casket was a photo of the
two of them, my dad and his sister, both beaming and so alive. Now she was
dead and he was clinging to life in a hospital 400 miles away.

When I was pulling into my garage after returning home from the
funeral, my cell phone rang. It was my mother on the other end. "He spoke
HE SPOKE!" I have never felt so much joy. A lab tech had come into his
room to draw blood. We had requested that, before doing anything to my
father, he be told what was being done. She announced that she was going
to draw his blood. He opened his eyes and looked at her and said, "What do
you want to do that for?"

This was the beginning of a very, very long road.

Six weeks had passed and my father seemed to float in and out of consciousness. When he did awaken, he would open up his big brown eyes whispering, "I love you" from a place that seemed so far away, I feared he would never return. One thing that had not been damaged was his gentle spirit and beautiful smile. By this time, we began to pay very close attention to what was being done for and to him. Along the way, it became increasingly clear that the Western medical system leaves a lot to be desired.

My father was transferred to a facility to be weaned off the ventilator, a machine that was breathing for him. We were given no choice in the matter. We did not understand why he was being transferred to another facility that seemed substandard at best, when he was in a hospital that was fully capable of caring for him and weaning him off the breathing machine. At this early point of navigating our way through the maze of the medical system, we did not know the correct questions to ask, and even if we did, we were somewhat afraid to do so.

After his transfer to this other facility, it became apparent that patient care was less than acceptable. We were forced to become very vocal about it. My nephew, who is a paramedic, searched the internet and found the home telephone number of the director of the facility. He made it clear that the following day he would contact every board of nursing and health he could find concerning the practices of the facility's nursing staff. And he did. At one point, one of my father's doctors, who was one of the few compassionate professionals involved in his care, took me aside after doing a daily routine examination and quietly said, "If your father has any hope at all, you need to get him out of here." He had just confirmed what I had known all along.

I went back to my parents' house and started searching through the phone book. I knew nothing of the town they lived in and had no contacts there. I looked up "brain injury" and found a clinic specializing in those services. Although the clinic was an outpatient facility, I decided to contact them anyway, figuring any help or information could be better than the situation I was currently facing. My father was nowhere near ready to not be in the hospital 24 hours a day. He was stable but still critical.

Through the outpatient clinic, I was referred to a caseworker, Mr. Lawrence Gamby, who was described as "the person" to be involved with in dealing with TBI. I phoned him, and he was willing to come to the hospital and meet with my mother and myself. He would be happy to take my father's case and help us navigate our way through this incredibly confusing process.

It is very hard to find anything that seems like a blessing when faced with something of this magnitude. However, I was able to find two—one in Mr. Gamby and another due to the fact that my parents were living in the state of Michigan at the time of the accident. Michigan has a no-fault insurance law as an option for insured motorists. If applicable, anyone involved in any motor vehicle accident is eligible to be covered by this insurance policy, if they have opted to pay extra for this coverage. Fortunately, my parents had carried the optimum coverage, so nearly all of the expenses related to my father's care were covered by this policy. This was truly a blessing, as his care ultimately ended up costing hundreds of thousands of dollars. Mr. Gamby's business was working as a patient advocate and he was instrumental in making sure my dad received the best care possible.

five

Calling All Angels

Through Mr. Gamby, I found The Rehabilitation Institute of Michigan (RIM) at Wayne State University. RIM is a traditional rehabilitation facility, and from all accounts, has one of the best neurological rehabilitation programs on the East Coast. A phone call was made to the head of the brain injury program there. He said it sounded as though my father did not meet the criteria to enter his program, but he would send someone out to the hospital to assess him. A caseworker from RIM came, assessed him, and told us she would let us know. We waited on pins and needles until the call came.

Indeed, my father did not meet all of the standard criteria to be admitted to RIM. There are certain methods used to measure projected outcomes with brain injury patients, such as The Glasgow Outcome, which is a scale using specific criteria and a point system to attempt to objectively determine the outcome of an individual with a TBI.

The Glasgow Outcome Scale:
1. **Dead**
2. **Vegetative State** *(meaning the patient is unresponsive, but alive; a "vegetable" in lay language)*
3. **Severely Disabled** *(conscious but the patient requires others for daily support due to disability)*
4. **Moderately Disabled** *(the patient is independent but disabled)*
5. **Good Recovery** *(the patient has resumed most normal activities but may have minor residual problems)*

In my experience, those methods and those alone are used to determine what the projected prognosis will be, ultimately determining if that person is even going to have a chance at becoming "rehabilitated." What about the human spirit? What about miracles? What about brain regeneration?

While the caseworker was visiting, my father was having a particularly good day. The nurses sat him up in a tilt chair before she arrived. To our amazement, while she was asking him questions, he was able to formulate a bit of a response. She had seen enough life in him to convince RIM to take a chance. He was transferred to RIM the next day.

The entire team at RIM came into my father's room shortly after he arrived. There were four or five doctors, all with different areas of expertise. My father was thoroughly examined. The head of the brain trauma unit echoed what we had been told all along—that with the severity of his injury, the chances were not good. At this point, I believe he was a two on the GOS. He then said they would do everything they could, giving him a shot at some sort of recovery, another miracle.

My father was at RIM for a total of 106 days, with my mother by his side. She slept on a cot next to his bed, only leaving when one of my brothers or my husband stayed overnight so she could go home and try to rest.

The therapy was intense. My father, much to everyone's surprise, started progressing rapidly. Physically, he made huge strides. Mentally, sometimes he knew who I was, while other times, he thought I was his mother or he did not know me at all, making it clear that he had a long way to go cognitively. But he did have many moments of lucidity, telling his old jokes, or making entertaining comments, which kept the staff in stitches. One day when I had arrived for one of my frequent visits, a therapist asked if he knew who I was, keeping with the routine of trying to stimulate his memory. His eyes lit up, he smiled and said, "Well that's my pride and joy!" I will never forget that day.

That was the Papa I knew. His memory may have been gone, but his spirit, his kindness, and his warmth could not be contained in a broken mind. He became a favorite of the nursing staff. The nurses told us that they requested to be assigned to his room on their shifts, and were extremely disappointed if their request was not granted. Somehow, though, they always seemed to end up in his room even when they were not assigned to him, just to check in or to hear a joke or two.

14

Throughout rehab, he relearned how to do everyday tasks that we all take for granted—how to use the toilet, wash himself, shave, put weight on his feet and help get himself from the wheelchair to the bed, and so on. He started eating again, although the feeding tube was left in as a precautionary measure.

On a beautiful day in May, he was released to go home. He was scheduled for outpatient rehab, to continue to learn how to walk and work toward improving his memory—another miracle.

six

Hope Interrupted

Unfortunately, this miracle was short-lived. He was at home for 10 days. One day he became very agitated, which was not my father's nature. This had happened a couple of times while he was in the hospital. His agitation always turned out to be caused by a urinary tract infection (UTI), something that he seemed to continuously develop due to the vast amounts of antibiotics he was being given. My mother called the doctor who had performed his surgery, since that hospital was nearest. She was instructed to bring him to the emergency room. I received a call from my aunt informing me of the situation. "Not the same emergency room where my brain-injured father was left sitting for three hours," I said. "Yes," she responded. I could only hope for the best.

I was finally able to reach my mother by phone to try and find out first hand what was going on. She told me that it seemed to be another UTI, and that they were going to admit him. "Is he still aggressive?" I asked. "No, honey, they have sedated him." "Sedated him?" I voiced my concern about a brain-injured patient being sedated. No worries, she consoled me, "The doctor says it's okay."

He had been in the hospital about three days when I arrived. It seemed as though every time he began to come out of sedation, they would decide that whichever sedative du jour that had been cast upon him was perhaps too strong due to my father's lack of responsiveness and they would take their chances on a different medication. To their credit, I can understand how they perceived this as being necessary. *(See diagram 2 for list of sedatives given.)*

I spent a night at the hospital with him, and he was uncontrollable. Even though he was in a very weakened state, my father was still very strong.

16

This particular night, he seemed to have developed superhuman strength. He was relentless in trying to get out of the bed. I was physically on the bed, trying to hold him down and begging him to relax, but he would have nothing to do with it. At one point, he became so agitated that he began to punch me, trying to get me to let him out of the bed. He wanted to go home and would focus on nothing else. Keep in mind, he could not walk and half of his skull was missing. One tiny fall would be detrimental. My father's brain injury was winning.

He was deteriorating very rapidly. I could no longer stand by and watch this unfold. I called RIM. "You need to get him back down here as soon as possible," was the response. "He should never have been sedated."

Doing a bit more research, I found that one of the sedatives he had been given clearly states in the physician's information that it is contraindicated for patients with TBI. It can cause Neuroleptic Malignant Syndrome (NMS), leading to catatonia, coma, and even death. There are no words to describe the complete and utter frustration I felt.

After being readmitted to RIM, the rehab team tried to return my father to his baseline functions, where he had been upon his release the first time. This was not to be. After six weeks with no signs of improvement, they decided that we needed to begin to make plans for his release. They strongly encouraged sending him to a nursing home. The thought of relinquishing my father to a nursing facility was unbearable and not an option that my family wanted to explore. I did, however, have the thought that at some point we may have no other choice, which led me to visit a few of the skilled nursing facilities. I could not fathom the idea of my father, who was 100 percent helpless and dependent on others, being left to the mercy of the unknown. For anyone who has ever had to make this decision, I need say no more. For anyone who has not, count this as one of your blessings.

At this time we decided that it would be best if we could move him closer to our family for the long road ahead and we proceeded with plans to get him to Ohio.

There was a new rehabilitation center that had just opened in the area that needed to fill its beds promptly. Thanks to this need, they were willing to admit my father on a trial basis. We had a small glimmer of hope as he was flown by Medi-Vac to Dayton Rehab in Ohio.

Once there, instead of showing the signs of improvement we had hoped for, he began to decline even more. It was obvious there was something terribly wrong one morning when I went to visit and he was weeping in terror, afraid to let anyone come near him. The rehab hospital staff believed this behavior was consistent with his brain injury. In response to my insisting that this was not typical of his past behavior, the staff relented and called for him to be taken to the emergency room. The tests revealed that he had another UTI and his electrolytes were completely abnormal. This was the beginning of another three-month hospitalization.

In my opinion, one very important piece of information was revealed during the transfer from the rehab to the hospital, during which his medications were stopped for over 20 hours. The morning following his hospital admittance, I walked into his room and he was sitting up in bed and smiling. This was a man who, 24 hours earlier, had been crying like a frightened animal.

I returned home that evening and began to research pharmaceuticals. It turned out to be a very enlightening experience in beginning to understand the side effects of medications. This was also a turning point in my life—I claimed a personal vendetta on pharmaceutical companies.

Please understand, I believe that there is a time and place for everything but the marketing of illness and use of prescription drugs in this country are out of control, and the health implications are frightening. Most other countries do not even allow the advertisement of pharmaceuticals on the air waves or in print media.

I realized that it must be the medication that was causing some, if not all, of what my father was experiencing. What I found was remarkable.

Not one, but seven of the medications had side effects my father was exhibiting. *(See diagram 2)*

I requested a meeting with his neurologists. They begrudgingly complied, and my husband and I spent the next several days before the scheduled meeting preparing for it. We created graphs that showed the medication side effects as well as the behaviors that he had been experiencing. During the meeting, the doctors made it clear that, in their opinion, the behavior was not caused by the side effects of the medications. One said, "In all of my 20 years of practice, I have never seen any patients exhibit these side effects." My question to him was, "Did you ever look?"

After much pleading, the doctor agreed to begin to wean him off all but the "most necessary" medications. In response, some of his symptoms slowly subsided. He had been diagnosed with many secondary complications due to the brain injury. After coming off the medications, many of the symptoms and complications disappeared. But sadly, the feeding tube once again became my father's only source of nutrition after he was sedated for the UTI in Michigan.

During this time, we became vigilant about his care, making sure someone stayed with him 24 hours a day. I believed it was a matter of life and death.

My father was on the hospital neuro unit. At one point, he lost his ability to digest the liquid food that was being given to him through his feeding tube on a continuous drip, 24 hours a day. This is known as "low motility." I had requested no new drugs be ordered until I had a chance to research the side effects, based on previous experience with his caregivers.

However, this request was not honored and, without my knowledge, his internist ordered a drug that was supposed to help with the condition of low motility.

Diagram 2

■ - Experiencing same symptoms as side effects of drugs

* - Sedatives given after Urinary Tract Infection

	Abnormal Dreams	Abnormal Thoughts	Aggression	Agitation	Anger	Anxiety	Apathy	Behavioral Changes	Breathing Problems	Catatonia	Confusion	Delusions	Dementia	Depression	Dizziness	Drowsiness	Fear
Ambien*	■	■	■	■		■	■	■	■		■	■	■	■	■	■	
Aranesp											■				■		
Aricept	■		■	■		■			■		■	■		■	■		
Ativan*	■	■	■	■		■		■			■			■	■	■	
Coreg		■							■					■	■		
Flomax									■						■	■	
Haldol*		■		■		■			■		■			■	■	■	
Imdur						■			■		■			■	■		
Keppra		■	■	■	■	■	■	■	■		■			■	■	■	
Lasix									■		■				■	■	
Levothyroxine						■			■								
Reglan		■		■		■			■		■			■	■	■	
Risperidone*	■	■	■	■		■	■		■	■	■			■	■	■	
Robitussin DAC*						■			■		■				■	■	
Xanax	■			■		■			■		■			■	■	■	■
Zocor	■			■		■			■			■		■			

Rough overview of patient symptoms cross-referenced with drug side effects.

Fatigue	Hallucinations	Headache	Hostility	Increased Libido	Irritability	Jitteriness	Memory Problems	Mood Changes	Muscular Rigidity	Nausea	Nervousness	Neuroleptic Malignant Syndrome	Restless	Renal Problems	Sleep Problems	Slurred Speech	Stomach Pain	Swelling	Tremors	UTI (Urinary Tract Infection)
■	■	■			■		■	■	■	■	■		■	■	■		■	■	■	■
■		■			■					■				■		■	■	■		
■	■	■	■	■	■				■	■	■	■	■	■	■		■	■	■	■
■	■	■	■		■		■	■	■	■	■	■	■		■		■		■	
■		■								■	■			■	■		■	■		
		■								■					■			■		
	■	■		■			■	■	■			■	■	■	■		■		■	
		■								■	■			■			■		■	■
■	■	■	■		■		■	■		■	■				■				■	■
		■							■	■			■				■			
■		■			■			■			■			■			■		■	
	■	■				■		■	■	■			■	■	■	■			■	■
■		■		■			■	■	■	■	■	■	■	■	■		■		■	■
	■	■						■		■	■		■		■		■		■	
■	■	■		■	■		■	■	■	■	■		■		■				■	
		■						■		■				■	■		■	■	■	■

I found out that my father had been given this new drug a couple of days after he had been started on it, and I immediately began to research it. This was a drug totally contraindicated for TBI, for it causes the same side effects (NMS) as the sedatives he had been given early on. I asked to speak with the internist concerning my discovery. Her answer was that she had to weigh the risk/benefit factor. There was another drug she could have ordered but didn't because it had the potential to cause diarrhea. NMS, which can possibly lead to coma or death, or diarrhea? Aghast at this seemingly insane situation, I was able to convince my mother to insist that the medication be changed immediately.

During this time period, I was well aware of the likely benefits acupuncture could have on my father's conditions. I found a "medical" acupuncturist, who also worked in the ER of the hospital where my father was, and once again requested permission from this hospital to treat my father. I contacted the physician directly and she seemed to think it would be no problem to treat him. She arranged to meet me in his room at 7:00 a.m. the following morning. She arrived outside his room, but did not come in. She called me out into the hall and said that there was too much red tape and that the hospital administrator would not give her permission to treat him. I expressed my frustration and, as she was leaving, she said, "I looked at your father's chart and it would be futile to treat him anyway. He has no qi." In TCM, qi is life force. If one has no qi, typically he or she is not alive.

I contacted my friend who is an acupuncturist locally. She is an amazing, loving, caring, and generous woman. She came to the hospital nightly to treat my father. We put a sign on the door that read "Family prayer service in progress" so that she could treat him without interruptions.

seven

What Happened to Home?

It had been another long road, but finally, after three months, my father was stable enough to be released from hospital care. The staff could not impress upon us enough how important it was for him to go to a nursing home. There were many meetings with the hospital social worker, which ended in frustration and tears. Again we decided against this, feeling deeply that if he had any chance of improvement, it would not be at a nursing home.

Moving forward with what would now be her new reality, my mother found a suitable apartment. My brothers and our extended family made the final heartbreaking trip to Michigan to pack up my parents' lives.

My father was returned to this new home with 24-hour-a-day nursing care. He was aware enough to know that something was amiss with this situation, as almost daily, he would plead to "go home." I can still hear those words, my father's frail voice, pleading, time after time, "I want to go home." In their new home, my parents, after over 50 years of marriage, had to have separate bedrooms because my dad could not be in a normal bed and required uninterrupted skilled nursing care.

If this situation was not so heartbreaking, I may have found it humorous at times. I remember one day when my mom had run an errand, a rare occurrence for her, as my father could not stand to be without her, even for a few moments. This particular day, he was sitting up in his hospital bed in his new room at his new home. Again pleading to go home, he was insistent that I start the car. Trying to somewhat control the situation and not let him become too upset, I obliged, starting the imaginary car. He proceeded to tell me to shut the door, go straight, turn left, turn right, and to stop at the imaginary lights. Our make-believe trip ended with my mother calling to check in. Once able to speak with her on the phone, he calmed down and fell into a deep sleep.

After moving to this new apartment from the hospital, he still showed no improvement. While there was great promise after the removal of many of the medications, his condition remained very weak, and for three months, he had a hard time fighting off recurring infections.

One day, while sitting and watching my father listless and lifeless and myself bored and out of reading materials, I picked up the can of liquid food that he had been living on for the majority of 18 months. This time I read the label. Looking at the ingredients, I realized there was nothing contained within this can to heal him. Theoretically, it was balanced, in the sense that it met all the RDA requirements, but I felt it was barely sustaining his life and doing nothing to heal him.

I had spent the past 20 years working in the health food industry. It was time to turn to what I knew, and so I began more research. I spent countless hours searching the internet, libraries, and health food stores. When looking for books, I searched for those with information on alternative healing, immediately turning to the index to see if the book had any information on brain injury.

While searching through a local health food store, I came across a book titled *Healing with Whole Foods,* by Paul Pitchford. Indeed it had information on brain injury. I was a bit overwhelmed by the book's size and the amount of information it contained, but I purchased it anyway. Upon returning home, I began to read through the book and could not put it down. The information was amazing, and the concept of utilizing food for healing spoke deeply to me. I felt like I had come home.

I immersed myself in *Healing with Whole Foods* and started to put together a feeding tube formula for my father, utilizing the foods recommended for not only my father's brain injury, but also the many secondary conditions with which he had been diagnosed.

I was quite familiar with whole foods, but this journey took me to a completely new level. I began to look at food as medicine. There were foods to clear mucus from his lungs; herbs and supplements that would improve his immune system; foods to help with his failing renal system and foods to guard against his consistent urinary tract infections.

During another visit with my acupuncturist, I told her of this fascinating book I had found and that I intended to create a feeding tube formula for my dad based on its information. She said that she had the book, that she had wanted to study with the author for years, and that he taught a course in Northern California.

With the inspiration of some of the information contained within *Healing with Whole Foods,* I was able to create a feeding tube formula for my father.

I was also able to contact Mr. Pitchford to schedule an appointment for a consultation about my father. I wanted him to examine the formula. He had amazing suggestions to improve upon what I had already developed as well as suggestions for additional Chinese herbs and various other supplements to enhance this concoction, all of which were very specific for brain injury.

eight

Into the Void

The hardest part of creating the feeding tube formula, which came to be known as "Liquid Hope," was finding a medical doctor who would support my efforts. I was fortunate enough to locate a local physician who agreed to oversee the process. Although Western-trained, he was open to alternative options. Before the doctor could begin to treat my father, he had to do a thorough examination. My father was wheeled into his office flat on a gurney, taken to the office by ambulance. He was almost non-responsive while being examined.

The doctor was willing to let me try this new approach slowly. We started replacing the canned food with my formula once a day. It seemed to be working well so we slowly transitioned until we were able to replace all of the canned formula with the homemade. Along with the feeding tube formula we prepared, we juiced daily, putting fresh vegetable juice down his feeding tube. In addition to the food formula, the juice blend we created also had extraordinarily specific ingredients to address his multitude of conditions. *(For juicing info, see pg. 48.)*

The difference was unbelievable. After one month, my father started coming back to life. About six weeks after receiving *only* my formulation, my father was taken back to the doctor for a follow-up appointment. This time, instead of being taken in on a gurney, my father was in a wheelchair. When the doctor appeared in the treatment room, my father, who only six weeks earlier, was in a near-comatose state, was sitting up and reached out his feeble hand for a handshake. After that visit, the doctor phoned me and said, "I want to tell you it is a miracle what you have done for your father." Without thinking about this, I replied, "It is not a miracle, it is simply nutrition."

At one point during one of his many hospitalizations, a speech therapist told us she was certain they would never be able to remove the feeding tube. Three months after he had been on the whole foods formula, the feeding tube was removed.

The food, combined with an alternative form of neurotherapy, provided by the Hahn-Hufford Center of Hope in Piqua, Ohio, proved very beneficial to my father. The Hahn-Hufford Center was founded by two women, Ruth Hahn and Gloria Hufford, who both had children with brain injuries and found no hope in traditional therapy and medicine.

They developed a technique known as tactile therapy, which stimulates the brain based on cellular memory. Started in the basement of a church in Piqua, Ohio, they have grown to a campus that provides brain rehabilitation for all age groups as well as the Nicholas School for special needs children. I honestly believe that the tactile therapy was instrumental in my father's cognitive improvement.

My father continues to have his ups and downs. He is seriously brain injured and is still very much a different man than he was before his accident. He has no short-term memory; he cannot remember his train of thought and has trouble finishing sentences. He cannot walk or play his guitar, once an appendage. Perhaps it is a blessing that he cannot remember what happened to him. With all of the challenges he faces, he has maintained dignity and superhuman tolerance to the daily pain he endures, as well as his gentle love for everyone around him.

Guarding what health he does have is a never-ending process. He recently suffered a huge setback when he contracted pneumonia. He was very ill and had no interest in eating. He became very weak and was sent back to the hospital where they re-inserted the feeding tube. Again my mother was sent home with a box full of canned food.

With assurance from my mother that she was not going to give the canned formula to him again, I resumed creating his whole foods formula, and once again, his recovery process was amazing.

As the journey continues, the outcome of this story is unknown, but I will never give up hope and will never quit fighting for my dad to have as much improvement and the best quality of life he can possibly have.

Did we make the right decision by not pulling the plug? This is a question without an absolute answer. What I do know is that I have had three years beyond what was expected with my father to tell him daily how much I love him. And I do know that when the time does come to let him go, I will have no regrets.

I remember one day during a very dark period I was experiencing, I was overwrought with emotions, overwhelmed and very, very distraught. I was talking on the phone to my aunt, one of my dad's sisters, and it was painfully clear that we both felt the end was drawing near for him. She said one remarkable sentence that could not have been more true. She told me, "where there is life, there is hope." She was right. My father fought back and pulled through again. He did not want to give up. It was beyond the imagination of anyone in our family that we would ever give up on him just as long as he was choosing to continue on.

I am sharing this very difficult story in hopes that others will be encouraged to hold on, believe in miracles, and never give up.

Epilogue

The previous chapters were written over 24 months ago. I write with a heavy heart that this story has come to an end. My father continued to fight hard.

Throughout the process, there were many caregivers involved in his care. One in particular did not know or want to know the value of whole foods and the nutrition plan that had been set forth for my father.

At the questioning of this very well-meaning licensed practical nurse (LPN), seeds of doubt began to enter my mother's mind. It is hard to embrace something that is foreign, especially in times of distress. Finally, trying to placate all involved and hoping for validation for my formula, I decided it was time to find a registered dietician (RD) to oversee the feeding tube formula process. Upon first meeting with this RD, she seemed to be supportive of the whole foods concept. However, she decided that his diet needed to be more nutrient-dense and began adding many ingredients that, from a holistic perspective, were hard on his organs, and his body could not process them properly.

He began to decline and became very congested. As a precautionary measure, a lung x-ray was taken, which revealed a small spot on his right lobe. His regular doctor was out of the country and an on-call doctor decided to place him on an antibiotic to make sure this did not turn into pneumonia. Again I researched the drug and I believed that the side effects were too much for my father's system.

Stated side effects:
- hypertension
- heart problems
- gastrointestinal bleeding
- kidney failure
- nightmares, hallucinations
- depression
- pulmonary embolism
- fever, chills
- edema (swelling) of the face, lips, neck, or hands

I immediately phoned my mother and the charge nurse, pleading that this drug not to be given to my dad. I had even found another option, an older antibiotic that had many less side effects. When I shared this, I was simply ignored by the pharmacist and the doctor. I was told there was absolutely no difference between the two and that both antibiotics were in the same class. The medication was given to my father as prescribed.

Four days later I awoke to a phone call from my mother with a message that they were in an ambulance on the way to the ER. I could hear my father screaming in pain in the background. He had gastrointestinal distress, and the nurse reported that she had found blood in the tube coming from his stomach. At the hospital, they performed routine tests and reported that they found "no significant" amounts of blood. They released him to return home with a prescription for an acid reflux drug and a 1000 mg. dose of Tylenol. They *released* him, even though for the four hours that he was in the ER, all of his vital signs were showing distress.

I was not there, but my mother reported that my dad looked up at the heavens and took one final breath. He died five hours after being released from the hospital.

His home health care nurses tell me they believe he died from a GI bleed, a side effect of the last antibiotic that had been prescribed. We will never know, as no autopsy was performed; my family chose to close the book on this sad, tragic story.

Unfortunately, most physicians today will tell you that in prescribing drugs, even *if* they are aware of all the side effects *(most aren't)*, they must weigh the risk/benefit factor. I wonder, if it were *their* loved one in the situation, would *they* then be so willing to take this risk?

The three years following my father's injury was a gift of unparalleled proportions for me personally. When he did pass, I could let him go, knowing that we did everything we possibly could for him. I said everything I needed to say and have no regrets that I did not have time to say goodbye. To be in his grace, to see how he endured things the human body should never have to endure, to see how even at his most weakened and fragile state, he still treated others with dignity, love, and respect. My father taught me as much about dying as he ever did about living.

Ten Things

1. **Take Care of Yourself Physically**

    It's easy to live on adrenaline but caregiver burnout is a very real thing. Ask for and accept help from friends and family. People generally are happy to help but often do not know what to do. Don't be afraid to ask for help when you need it. Get a support system in place early on; it will help immensely.

2. **Take Care of Yourself Emotionally**

    Many times, depending on the nature of the illness or injury, it will change everyone's life forever. This can happen very suddenly. Watch for signs of depression, and don't delay in getting professional help when you need it. We often feel guilty doing anything pleasurable for ourselves when we see our loved one suffering. It is important to find a place for these feelings when they arise.

3. **Find an Advocate**

    I am convinced there needs to be a patient advocate for anyone undergoing extensive treatment in a medical institution. I'm not talking about an advocate the hospital offers. I recommend an individual who is not afraid to ask tough questions, do the required research and who will not take "no" for an answer. Make sure that you are completely comfortable with the answers you are being given. If you are not satisfied with the information you are receiving, you may want to dig a little deeper. This is not an easy task and may be very time consuming. It is in everyone's best interest if you delegate this day-to-day task to someone you trust until the situation is resolved. This could be a family member, friend or a casual acquaintance who has personally experienced getting caught up in the medical maze and has figured out how to navigate the murky waters.

4. **Keep Copious Notes**

    You will need to call employers, insurance carriers, friends, family, or even maybe an attorney, etc. Be sure to jot down notes during your calls.

As you move through the process, you may forget what you were told, or how you were supposed to follow up on the information you received.

5. **Journal Daily**

This will give you something to do as you may possibly face many hours of endless waiting. In general, journaling is one of the most therapeutic things anyone can do. One of the numerous benefits of journaling is that you are actually getting things out of your head, if even momentarily, allowing yourself a space to breathe into. The reprieve may be temporary but it does help. Also, when faced with a situation such as this, it serves as a chronicle of days, times, and events. Under stress, we sometimes move through events in a fog-like state, losing all connections with time and space. It is imperative that you record everything that happens during this time.

6. **Request To Be Notified of Any Change in Medication**

There are always many different specialists involved in any patient's care. It is easy for them to overlook an existing medication, which may have a dangerous interaction with the new medication ordered. In Traumatic Brain Injury in particular, patients are more susceptible to side effects and may react adversely to some pharmacological agents.[1]

7. **Do Your Own Research**

Many medications have side effects worse than the condition that the drug is supposed to be treating. Research this for yourself on sites such as drugs.com under the "professional information." You will find information there that you will generally not receive from doctors or pharmacists. Doctors say they "have to weigh the benefits against the risks." If this is not an acceptable answer, and if you are not comfortable with the risks, you do have the right to refuse the medication *(see Patient's Bill of Rights, pg. 35)*. Typically older medications have less side effects than the new "designer" drugs. Also, ask what medication is medically necessary to achieve the desired outcome. Many times it seems that medication is prescribed simply because it can be. In my experience, patients or their families are never informed of the possible side effects. When questioned, many doctors will also tell you that when the medication was tested before market release, only one or two percent of people in the trials experienced the side effects. What they do not tell you is that many of those trials were only done on as few as 70 people. With many of the drugs these days having potentially deadly side effects, is even the reported 1% worth the risk?

8. Be Positive

Remember, no negative talk. Many people, including a lot of doctors, are under the impression that patients in an unconscious state do not know what is going on around them. Every brain injury is unique and it is unknown how aware the person in a coma is. Some people remember very vividly what was going on around them while they were in a coma. Other people do not. A study in the *New England Journal of Medicine* shows that scans can detect signs of awareness in patients thought to be closed off from the world. In the study, released Feb. 2010, they asked comatose patients and healthy volunteers to imagine playing tennis while they were being scanned. In both populations, this stimulated activity in the pre-motor cortex, part of the brain that deals with movement.[2]

9. Act Naturally

This is hard to do, but necessary. Read to your loved one—newspapers, favorite books, letters, and cards. Tell the patient daily what month, day, and year it is. Tell them about everything positive that has happened in your day and any milestones. I know there is nothing about your world that seems like it will ever be normal again, but by projecting faith instead of fear, both you and your loved one will benefit on some level.

10. Auditory Stimulation

Bring in a CD player and play the patient's favorite music. Research has shown positive effects on awake patients undergoing evaluation for brain surgery.[3] It would make sense that auditory stimulation would have the same effects on the cerebral cortex of comatose patients.

Patient's Bill of Rights

The American Hospital Association
A Patient's Bill of Rights
Another person chosen by the patient can exercise these rights on the patient's behalf. A proxy decision maker can exercise these rights if the patient lacks decision-making ability, is legally incompetent, or is a minor.

- The patient has the right to considerate and respectful care.

- The patient has the right to and is encouraged to obtain from doctors and other direct caregivers appropriate, current, and understandable information about diagnosis, treatment, and prognosis. Except in emergencies when the patient lacks decision-making ability and the need for treatment is urgent, the patient is entitled to the chance to discuss and request information about the specific procedures and/or treatments, the risks involved, the possible length of recuperation, and the medically reasonable alternatives and their risks and benefits. Patients have the right to know the identity of doctors, nurses, and others involved in their care, as well as when those involved are students, patients, or other trainees. The patient also has the right to know the immediate and long-term financial implications of treatment choices, insofar as they are known.

- The patient has the right to make decisions about the plan of care before and during treatment. The patient has the right to refuse a recommended treatment or plan of care to the extent allowed by law and hospital policy and to be informed of the medical consequences of this action. In case of refusal, the patient is entitled to other appropriate care and services that the hospital provides or transfers to another hospital. The hospital should notify patients of any policy that might affect patient choice within the institution.

- The patient has the right to have an advance directive (such as a living will, health care proxy, or durable power of attorney for health care) concerning treatment or designating a surrogate decision maker with the expectation that the hospital will honor the intent of that directive to the extent permitted by law and hospital policy. Health care institutions must tell patients of their rights under state law and hospital policy to make informed medical choices, ask if the patient has an advance directive, and include that information in patient records. The patient has the right to timely information about hospital policy that may limit its ability to implement fully a legally valid advance directive.

- The patient has the right to every consideration of privacy. Case discussion, consultation, examination, and treatment should be conducted so as to protect each patient's privacy.

- The patient has the right to expect that all communications and records related to his/her care will be treated as confidential by the hospital, except in cases such as suspected abuse and public health hazards when reporting is permitted or required by law. The patient has the right to expect that the hospital will stress the confidentiality of this information when it releases it to any other parties entitled to review information in these records.

- The patient has the right to review the records about his/her care and to have the information explained or interpreted as necessary, except when restricted by law.

- The patient has the right to expect that, within its capacity and policies, a hospital will make reasonable response to a patient's request for appropriate and medically indicated care and services. The hospital must provide evaluation, service, and/or referral as indicated by the urgency of the case. When medically appropriate and legally permitted, or when a patient has requested, a patient may be transferred to another facility. The institution to which the patient is to be transferred must first have accepted the patient for transfer. The patient must also have the benefit of complete information and explanation concerning the need for, risks, benefits, and alternatives to such a transfer.

- The patient has the right to ask and be informed of business relationships among the hospital, educational institutions, other health care providers, or payers that may influence the patient's treatment and care.

- The patient has the right to consent to or decline to take part in research studies or human experimentation affecting care and treatment or requiring direct patient involvement, and to have those studies fully explained prior to consent. A patient who declines to take part in research or experimentation is entitled to the most effective care that the hospital can otherwise provide.

- The patient has the right to expect reasonable continuity of care when appropriate and to be informed by doctors and other caregivers of available and realistic patient care options when hospital care is no longer appropriate.

- The patient has the right to be informed of hospital policies and practices that relate to patient care treatment, and responsibilities. The patient has the right to be informed of available resources for resolving disputes, grievances, and conflicts, such as ethics committees,patient representatives, or other mechanisms available in the institution. The patient has the right to be informed of the hospital's charges for services and available payment methods.

Patient Responsibilities

The partnership nature of health care requires that patients, or their families/ surrogates, take part in their care. The effectiveness of care and patient satisfaction with the treatment depends, in part, on the patient fulfilling certain responsibilities. The following are patient responsibilities:

- Patients are responsible for providing information about past illnesses, hospitalizations, medications, and other matters related to health status. To participate effectively in decision-making, patients are to take responsible for asking for additional information or explanation about their health status or treatment when they do not fully understand information and instructions.

- Patients are also responsible for ensuring that the health care institution has a copy of their written advance directive if they have one.

- Patients are responsible for telling their doctors and other caregivers if they expect problems in following prescribed treatment.

- Patients should be aware of the hospital's duty to be reasonably efficient and fair in providing care to other patients and the community. The hospital's rules and regulations are intended to help the hospital meet this responsibility. Patients and their families are responsible for making reasonable accommodations to the needs of the hospital, other patients, medical staff, and hospital employees.

- Patients are responsible for giving necessary information for insurance claims and for working with the hospital to make payment arrangements, when necessary.

- A person's health depends on much more than health care services. Patients are responsible for recognizing the impact of their lifestyle on their personal health.

Reference: http://www.aha.org

Supplemental Nutrition

The supplements listed below were utilized in conjunction with the whole foods tube feeding formula.

Phosphatidyl Choline w/Folic Acid & B12

Phosphatidylcholine: It appears both ways here. Lecithin known as phosphatidylcholine is also known as lecithin, although lecithin is also a term loosely applied to describe a combination of phosphatidylcholine with other phospholipids. Most people normally ingest 3 to 6 grams of lecithin a day through eggs, soy, and meats. Vegetables, fruits and grains contain very little lecithin.

Phosphatidylcholine is the most abundant phospholipid component in all cells. Phosphatidylcholine levels in brain cell membranes decline with age, perhaps contributing to memory loss. Several studies have been done with phosphatidylcholine to investigate its effects on memory. The results of the studies have not been consistent. Some have shown positive responses, while others have shown no difference in memory or learning after lecithin administration. Phosphatidylcholine has even been evaluated in Parkinson's disease. In this nine-week long double-blind study, sixteen elderly patients took a daily dose of approximately 32 grams of a commercial lecithin preparation. Marked clinical improvement was not observed, but there was a slight improvement in memory, cognition, and motility.[4]

Folic Acid: Folic acid does appear to decrease chances of people getting high blood pressure because it relaxes blood vessels. Due to lower blood pressure, the supplement may be indicated as good stroke prevention. It also may act to reduce signs of aging by helping people to retain memory and mental acuity.

It may have a role in regulating mood, especially when taken with other B vitamins. It reduces homocysteine levels, which are found in greater amount in depressed people. Yet whether folic acid alone is capable of fully ending depression is not proven.

B12: In combination with other B-group vitamins, vitamin B12 ensures the smooth functioning of vital life processes of the human body. It is important for maintaining a healthy nervous system and DNA production. Vitamin B12 helps to regulate the formation of red blood cells in the body. Other benefits of vitamin B12 include its role in maintaining and increasing energy levels in the human body.

Mental Clarity™ w/Lion's Mane

Mental Clarity™ features MycoMedicinals® Lion's Mane, Hericium erinaceus, the most important mushroom for supporting brain function. Japanese research has shown that Lion's Mane produces compounds called Eninacines, which are strong stimulators to nerve growth factor synthesis. These compounds stimulate neurons to regrow, which support normal cognitive function, muscular coordination and response, and neurological repair.

Silica

During the 20th century, progress was made by pioneering researchers and scientists such as Carlisle, Butenandt, Iler, Bergna, Kervran, and Schwartz. Edith Carlisle's work in the 70's through the 90's at the UCLA School of Public Health, perhaps more than any other, demonstrated the necessity of having silica in the body for proper growth and development. As a result of her research, we know that silica is absolutely essential for the body to create and maintain collagen. What was dramatically shown through Carlisle's research was that when silica is withheld from normal nutrition, gross abnormalities develop and normal growth does not take place. While Carlisle's work was done with chickens and mice, humans have also been experimenting with silica.[5]

Turmeric w/Bromelin

Turmeric: The antioxidant/anti-inflammatory compounds in turmeric are a group of polyphenols called *curcuminoids*, named for the best known among them, **curcumin.** In a recent laboratory study at the University of Illinois, researchers tested nine curcuminoids isolated from turmeric root for their ability to protect cultured rat cells from damage caused by *amyloid-beta* (also called beta-amyloid); this small protein molecule is the principal constituent, along with some polysaccharides, of the senile plaques found in the brains of Alzheimer's victims.[6] Amyloid-beta is believed to be formed in part through oxidative damage caused by free radicals, and it causes further free radical production, causing further oxidative damage, etc. Amyloid-beta is neurotoxic—it kills neurons.

In addition, it plays a role in the formation of neurofibrillary tangles, its evil, neurotoxic twin in the pathology of Alzheimer's. All this death and destruction occurs primarily in cholinergic neurons (those for which acetylcholine is the neurotransmitter) in certain regions of the brain, notably the hippocampus, which govern vital aspects of memory and other cognitive functions.

A study[7] published in the *Italian Journal of Biochemistry* discussed curcumin's role in the induction of the heme oxygenase pathway, a protective system that, when triggered in brain tissue, causes the production of the potent antioxidant bilirubin, which protects the brain against oxidative (free radical) injury. Such oxidation is thought to be a major factor in aging and to be responsible for neuro degenerative disorders including dementias like Alzheimer's disease. Another study[8] conducted jointly by an Italian and U.S. team and presented at the American Physiological Society's 2004 annual conference in Washington, DC, confirmed that curcumin strongly induces expression of the gene, called hemeoxygenase-1 (HO-1) in astrocytes from the hippocampal region of the brain.

Bromelin: Found in Pineapple, this fragrant tropical fruit is rich in a compound called bromelain. Some experts believe that turmeric and bromelain mixed together have a singularly powerful effect.

Oil of Oregano

Oregano Oil is Antibacterial and Antimicrobial According to a recent study[9] published in the *Journal of Agricultural and Food Chemistry,* one of the most promising oregano oil benefits is its high antimicrobial and antibacterial activity. This is believed to be caused by its high content of flavanoids, or secondary plant metabolites known for their antioxidant activity. In addition, the study found that oregano essential oil has antimicrobial properties which can counteract food borne pathogens, such as Listeria monocytogenes, which is responsible for the lethal illness, listeriosis. Both the antibacterial and antimicrobial benefits of oil of oregano can be useful in restoring health, and possibly in food preservation.

Oregano Oil as a Anti-Parasitic: Oregano oil has been used to effectively treat internal parasites, including Blastocystis hominis, a small parasite that infects the intestinal tracts of humans. A study[10] published in *Phytotherapy Research* found that oral administration of oregano oil caused a disappearance of parasite activity in most patients, as well as an improvement of gastrointestinal symptoms. Other patients experienced a significant decline in the number of parasites over the course of the study.

Chlorella

Chorella has shown to be one of the greatest food substances for cleansing the bowel, liver, blood and other elimination systems. Chlorophyll, is found in all green vegetables, especially the green, leafy vegetables. Food greens contain less than half of one percent chlorophyll. Alfalfa, from which chlorophyll is commercially extracted, has only 8 or 9 pounds per ton, about 0.2% when extracted, and alfalfa is one of the plants highest in chlorophyll. Commercial liquid chlorophyll often contains only about 1% chlorophyll. Green algae are the highest sources of chlorophyll in the plant world; and, of all the green algae studied so far, chlorella is the highest, often ranging from 3 to 5% chlorophyll.' Chlorella supplements can speed up the rate of cleansing of the bowel, bloodstream and liver, by supplying plenty of chlorophyll. In addition, the mysterious Chlorella Growth Factor (CGF) speeds up the healing rate of any damaged tissue.

Experiments have been done in the Republic of China, Japan, and Germany to see what effects chlorella would have in preventing or reversing various liver conditions, and the results are promising and exciting. One of the first comparative studies of the effects of alga and other foods (skim milk powder and cooked egg white) on the liver was done in the early 1950s in Germany at the universities of Bonn and Cologne. Dr. Hermann Fink fed groups of rats single-food diets to see how alga compared with known food substances. On a diet of only skim milk, most of the rats died of liver necrosis, while one rat on the egg white diet showed signs of necrosis. All rats on the alga diet remained healthy. Dr. Fink concluded that further research should be done to find out if green alga had therapeutic value for the liver.[11]

Primal Defense Probiotic
Latro Flora Powder Probiotic™

Primal Defense uses "superfoods" such as spirulina, chlorella, wheat grass and alfalfa grass, along with probiotics. *Garden of Life* states that Primal Defense supports the proper balance of friendly and potentially harmful bacteria in the gastrointestinal system. This balance maintains a healthy gastrointestinal environment when other factors may disrupt the bacterial balance.[12] Taking antibiotics, for instance, kills friendly bacteria as well as harmful bacteria, and fungi, parasites and an overabundance of yeast can also upset the balance, according to the U.S. National Institutes of Health (NIH).[13]

Milk Thistle

Liver regeneration is the most documented benefit of milk thistle. The plant is actually the most researched and best understood of all the medicinal herbs. In fact, study after study has confirmed its most significant property: namely, the ability to protect and actually regenerate the liver with new cells. Laboratory studies suggest that milk thistle may benefit the liver by protecting and promoting the growth of liver cells, fighting oxidation (a chemical process that can damage cells), and inhibiting inflammation.[14]

Green Tea Extract

In a study with 42,093 Japanese individuals 2,774 people, or 6.6 percent of the study population, suffered from psychological stress, and green tea consumption was said to improve psychological well-being. Researchers led by Atsushi Hozawa from the Tohoku University Graduate School of Medicine report their findings online in the *American Journal of Clinical Nutrition*. Findings: A higher consumption of green tea is associated with a lower prevalence of cognitive impairment in humans.[15]

CoQ10

In the *Journal of Nutritional and Environmental Medicine*[16], CoQ10 research pioneers Drs. Ram Singh and Adarsh Kumar reported the results of a very well-designed trial indicating CoQ10 might have a powerful role as adjunctive therapy in patients with end-stage kidney disease—in some cases even reducing or averting the need for dialysis. In a randomized, double-blind, placebo-controlled trial, the researchers found CoQ10 treatment decreased progression and reversed renal dysfunction in a majority of patients with end-stage disease, many of whom were able to discontinue dialysis over the course of the 12-week trial. The report followed up on a pilot study the scientists published in 2000 involving a smaller number of subjects. End-stage kidney disease produces marked organ contraction and progressive dysfunction, with corresponding increases in levels of serum creatinine and blood urea nitrogen. Levels of toxic waste products accumulate in the blood because the kidneys cannot clear them from the body. Dr. Singh and his colleagues documented significantly lower levels of serum creatinine and blood urea nitrogen in the CoQ10-treated patients, with increases in creatinine clearance and urine output regardless of patient dialysis or baseline status. More significantly, only half the number of CoQ10 patients required dialysis at the end of the study when compared to subjects receiving placebo.

Essiac Tea

Essiac is a tea that is widely known as a homeopathic cancer treatment. It is prepared from a mixture of four herbs—Arctium lappa, Rumex acetosella, Ulmus rubra and Rheum officinale, of which each have been reported to possess antioxidant and anti-cancer activity. Essiac itself has also been reported to demonstrate anti-cancer activity in vitro, although its effects in vivo are still controversial. In a study[17] Leonard et al used concentrations of 5, 10, 25, and 50% to examine the effects of Essiac on free radical scavenging and DNA damage in a non-cellular system, as lipid peroxidation using the RAW 264.7 cell line. It was observed that Essiac effectively scavenged hydroxyl, with the 50% tea preparation reducing radical signal up to 84% and superoxide radicals up to 82%. In addition, the 50% concentration prevented hydroxyl radical-induced DNA damage and inhibited hydroxyl radical-induced lipid peroxidation by up to 50%. The study states that these results indicate that "Essiac tea possesses potent antioxidant and DNA-protective activity, properties that are common to natural anti-cancer agents" and that this study is significant because it provides data to help explain the mechanisms behind Essiac's reported anti-cancer effects.

Nattokinase

Nattokinase is a potent fibrinolytic (anti-clotting) enzyme complex extracted and highly purified from a traditional Japanese food called Natto. Natto is a fermented cheese-like food that has been used in Japanese culture for more than 1,000 years for its popular taste, and as a folk remedy for heart and vascular diseases. Research[18, 19, 20] has shown that Nattokinase supports the body in breaking up and dissolving the unhealthy coagulation of blood. In fact, it has been shown to have four times greater fibrinolytic activity than plasmin.

Red Marine Algae *(Gigartina skottsbergii)*

Red marine algae has been a valued food in Asia for many of years due to its high nutritious value and trace mineral qualities. Red marine algae has been used by people as a food staple for thousands of years in costal regions around the world. This alga is a rich source of vitamins, minerals, proteins, complex carbohydrates, enzymes, essential fatty acids, fiber and trace elements.

Red Marine Algae's medicinal properties are thought to enhance the immune system's response, indicating that it is an immuno modulatory perfect as an antiviral agent. The polysaccharides or long chained complex sugars stimulate interferon production as well as other anti-tumor and immune enhancing agents such as T and B cells, improving their action in the body.

The present data[21] shows that the red microalgal polysaccharides profoundly inhibited retroviral malignant cell transformation and retrovirus replication. Most effective inhibitory activity of these polysaccarides on cell transformation was obtained when the cells were treated with polysaccharide before or at the time of infection. These results support the possibility that at least part of the inhibitory effect of the polysaccharide was due to blocking some of the viral receptors, thus interfering with the penetration of the virus into the cells. On the other hand, the reversibility of this inhibitory activity strongly suggests that the polysaccharide exerted its inhibitory effect also on a certain event occurring after proviral integration. Thus, it appears that Porphyridium sp. polysaccharide has a pleiotropic mode of action during the infection cycle of MuSV. The exact steps (or step) during the viral replication cycle that are affected by Porphyridium sp. polysaccharide remain to be elucidated.

Clinical trials have shown that these sulfated polysaccharides can suppress HIV, herpes, and influenza viruses, and patients have reported a lessening or even a halting of viral growth within the body.

In addition to antiviral properties, red marine algae have been useful in weight-loss, lowering cholesterol and fat in the blood, and detoxifying and counteracting degenerative conditions. The antiviral polysaccharides found in red algae can stimulate the production of interferons, which work with the immune system and strengthen it. A long series of scientific studies has confirmed that red marine algae have potent antiviral applications and that, when used as a medicinal food, could play and important role for people who are susceptible to herpes (cold sore) conditions, including genital herpes and shingles, as well as other viral conditions.

Holy Basil

David Winston, herbalist uses Holy Basil in clinical practice to enhance cerebral circulation and memory. It can be combined with other cerebral stimulants such as rosemary, bacopa, and ginkgo to help people with menopausal cloudy thinking, poor memory, attention deficit disorder (ADD) and attention deficit hyperactivity disorder (ADHD) and to speed up recovery from head trauma.

Dr. Satish Kulkarni's studies found that Holy basil has many medicinal properties. The leaves are included in most of the herbal nervo-tonics. A fresh juice/decoction of holy basil with a few other herbs is taken for improving memory. The herb can be tried in conditions like Alzheimer and alcohol brain syndrome which are modern diseases and until now there have been no perfect remedies for these disorders. I, myself have given a clinical trial of this herb for the patient who complained partial loss of memory after accident and observed miraculous results. Systemic clinical trials under medical supervision may give a valuable gift to medical science and patients suffering from loss of memory may be benefited.[22]

What We Juiced

Chinese nutrition uniquely differs from modern Western nutrition in that it determines the energetic and therapeutic properties of foods rather than analyzing them solely according to their chemical constituents.

When looking at Food as Medicine, all the ingredients that we used for juicing daily have numerous health benefits. The properties listed below are the healing properties we were utilizing them for to address specific health conditions that my father experienced.

Daikon Radish
Removes stagnant food, moistens lungs, resolves mucus clearing congestion.

Carrots
Detoxifying, strengthening of all organs, lubrication of the intestines.

Celery
Tonifying of kidneys, stops bleeding, strengthens spleen and stomach.

Beets
Nourishes the blood, tonifies the heart, calms the spirit, lubricating to the intestines, cleanses the liver.

Garlic
Antimicrobial actions. Raw garlic has the ability to kill a wide variety of microorganisms by direct contact, including fungi, bacteria, viruses and protozoa.

Ginger

Calms upset stomachs, soothes nausea and stops diarrhea. Ginger is well known in Chinese medicine for its usefulness in cutting through phlegm in the lungs, helping to ventilate lungs.

Wheatgrass

Offers the benefits of a liquid oxygen transfusion since the juice contains liquid oxygen. Oxygen is vital to many body processes: it stimulates digestion (the oxidation of food), promotes clearer thinking (the brain utilizes 25% of the body's oxygen supply), and protects the blood against anaerobic bacteria. Cancer cells cannot exist in the presence of oxygen.

Resource Guide

Neurological Facilities

Hahn-Hufford Center for Hope
Rehabilitation Center for Neurological Development
1306 Garbry Road
Piqua, OH 45356
Website: www.rcnd.org
937-773-7630
Carla Bertke, Executive Director

RIM
Rehabilitation Institute of Michigan
261 Mack Avenue
Detroit, MI 48201
Website: www.rimrehab.org
313-745-1203
William H. Restum, PhD, President

Healing Food

Functional Formularies
Customized Organic Whole Foods Meal Replacement
Website: www.functionalformularies.com
937-271-0381
Lynn Goldstein R.D. N.D.
Robin Gentry McGee CHHP

Integrative Studies

Bastyr University
14500 Juanita Dr. NE
Kenmore, WA 98028
Website: www.bastyr.edu
425-425-3110

Center for Mind Body Medicine
5225 Connecticut Ave. N.W.
Suite 415
Washington, D.C. 20015
Website: www.cmbm.org
202-966-7338
Dr. James S. Gordon, Founder/Director

Distance Learning
Institute for Integrative Nutrition
Website:www.integrativenutrition.com
877-730-5444
Joshua Rosenthol, Founder/Director

Books
Healing with Whole Foods: Asian Traditions and Modern Nutrition
North Atlantic Books, 2003
Website: www.healingwithwholefoods.com
Paul Pitchford, Author

Informational Websites
WHO
World Health Organization
Website: www.who.int

ITM
Institute for Traditional Healing
Website: www.itmonline.org
Subhuti Dharmananda, Founder/Director

Physcians Committee for Responsible Medicine (PCRM)
5100 Wisconsin Ave., N.W.
Suite 400
Washington, D.C. 20016
Website: www.pcrm.org
202-686-2210
Dr. Neal Barnard, Founder/Director

The Health Ranger
Website: www.healthranger.org
Mike Adams, Founder

Environmental Working Group
Website: www.ewg.org

Acknowledgements

I am thankful and grateful to my family, my mother and brothers who completely supported me even though I know it was hard for them at times. To my husband who never questioned my immersion into the process of healing and who totally supported the continuation of my education.

To all of my friends far and wide who cheered me on and have never stopped believing in me.

References

1. National Institutes of Health. National Institutes of Health Consensus Development Conference Statement: Rehabilitation of Persons with Traumatic Brain Injury October 26-28, 1998. National Institute of Child Health and Human Development. http://www.nichd.nih.gov/publications/pubs/TBI_1999/NIH_Consensus_Statement.cfm. Published March 9, 1999. Accessed May 2010.

2. Rao S. MRI Brain Scan Shows Signs of Some Consciousness in "Vegetative" Patients. Discover: Science, Technology, and The Future. http://blogs.discovermagazine.com/80beats/2010/02/04/mri-brain-scans-show-signs-of-consciousness-in-some-vegetative-patients/. Published February 4th, 2010. Accessed May 2010.

3. Lesser RP, Lee HW, Webber WRS, Prince B, Crone NE, Miglioretti DL. Short-term variations in response to distribution to cortical stimulation. Brain. 2008;131(6):1528-1531. Doi:10.1093/brain/awn044.

4. Sahelian R, MD. Phospatidylcholine supplement health benefit and medical uses. Dr. Ray Sahelian, M.D. http://www.raysahelian.com/phospha.html. Published 2005. Accessed May 2010.

5. Lavdas AA, Matsas R. Towards personalized cell-replacement therapies for brain repair. Per Med. 2009;6(3):293-313.

6. Park SY, Kim DSHL. Discovery of natural products from Curcuma longa that protect cells from amyloid-beta insult: a drug discovery effort against Alzheimer's disease. J Nat Prod. 2002;65(9):1227-1231.

7. Calabrese V, Butterfield DA, Stella AM. Nutritional antioxidants and the heme oxygenase pathway of stress tolerance: novel targets for neuroprotection in Alzheimer's disease. Ital J Biochem. 2003;52(4):177-181.

8. The George Metaljan Foundation. Tumeric. The World's Healthiest Foods.http://www.whfoods.com/genpage.php?tname=foodspice &dbid=78. Updated 2010. Accessed May 2010.

9. Viuda-Martos M, Ruiz-Navajas Y, Fernández-López J, Pérez-Álvarez JA. Antibacterial activity of different essential oils obtained from spices widely used in Mediterranean diet. J Agric Food Chem. 2008;43(3): 526-531.

10. Force M, Sparks WS, Ronzio RA. Inhibition of enteric parasites by emulsified oil of oregano in vivo. Phytother Res. 2000;14(3):213-214.

11. Merchant RE, Andre CA. A review of recent clinical trials of the nutritional supplement Chlorella phrenoidosa in the treatment of fibromyalgia, hypertension, and ulcerative colitis. Altern Ther Health Med. 2001;7(3):79-91.

12. Garden of Life. Primal Defense HSO Probiotic Formula. Garden of Life: Empowering Extraordinary Health. http://www.gardenoflife.com/ ProductsforLife/SUPPLEMENTS/DigestiveHealth/PrimalDefense/ tabid/638/Default.aspx. Updated 2010. Accessed May 2010. Replacement for Mitra, Rolfe, Dunne, Gill

13. National Institute of Health. An introduction to probiotics. National Center for Complementary and Alternative Medicine. http://nccam.nih. gov/health/probiotics/. Published January 2007. Updated August 2008. Accessed May 2010. Replacement for Mitra, Rolfe, Dunne, Gill

14. National Institute of Health. CAM and Hepatitis C: a focus on herbal supplements. National Center for Complementary and Alternative Medicine. http://nccam.nih.gov/health/hepatitisc. Published October 2008. Updated October 2009. Accessed May 2010.

15. Kuriyama S et al. Green tea consumption and cognitive function: a cross-sectional study from the Tsurugaya Project. Am J Clin Nutr. 2006;83(2):355-361.

16. Singh RB, Kumar A. Randomized, double-blind, placebo-controlled trial of coenzyme Q10 in patients with end-stage renal failure. J Nutr Environ Med. 2003;13(1):13-22.

17. Leonard SS, Keil D, Mehlman T, Proper S, Shi X, Harris GK. Essiac tea: Scavenging of reactive oxygen species and effects on DNA damage. J Ethnopharmocol. 2006; 103(2):288-296.

18. Suzuki Y, Kondo K, Ichise H, Tsukamoto Y, Urano T, Umemura K. Dietary supplementation with fermented soybeans suppresses intimal thickening. Nutrition. 2003;19(3):261-264.

19. Sumi, H. et al. Enhancement of the fibrinolytic activity in plasma by oral administration of nattokinase. Acta haematol. 1990; 84:139-43.

20. Suzuki Y et al. Dietary supplementation of fermented soybean, natto, suppresses intimal thickening and modulates the lysis of mural thrombi after endothelial injury in rat femoral artery. Life Sci. 2003;73(10): 1289-1298.

21. Talyshinsky MM, Souprun YY, Huleihel MM. Anti-viral activity of red microalgal polysaccharides against retroviruses. Cancer Cell Int. 2002;2:8.

22. Kulkarni S, MD, Holy basil taken for improving memory. Dr. Satish Kulkarni, satishvk@hotmail.com, http://www.nzhealth.net.nz/herbs/holybasil.shtml

60467289R00040

Made in the USA
Middletown, DE
30 December 2017